God Always Cares

Published by Standard Publishing, Cincinnati, Ohio
www.standardpub.com

Copyright © 2003, 2007 by Standard Publishing. All rights reserved. #15308. Manufactured in Cincinnati, OH, USA, May 2010. Happy Day logo and trade dress are trademarks of Standard Publishing. Printed in the United States of America. Illustrated by Kathryn Marlin. All Scripture quotations, unless otherwise indicated, are taken from the *International Children's Bible*®. Copyright © 1986, 1988, 1999, 2005 by Thomas Nelson, Inc. Used by permission. All rights reserved. Reproducible: Permission is granted to reproduce these pages for ministry purposes only—not for resale.

ISBN-13: 978-0-7847-2001-1
ISBN-10: 0-7847-2001-0

15 14 13 12 11 10   2 3 4 5 6 7 8 9 10

Cincinnati, Ohio

God always cares.

"He cares for you." *1 Peter 5:7*

Flowers blooming in my yard,

New leaves budding on my tree . . .

Those are ways my Father shows

That he always cares for me.

When I gaze at a starry sky,

Or when I play beside the sea,

God is with me all the time

Because he always cares for me.

Dear God, I'm very glad to know

That you are watching over me.

I will trust you all my life

Because you always care for me.

"Your Father knows the things you need." *Matthew 6:8*